MERRY CHRISTMAS

Satomi Ichikawa

MERRY CHRISTMAS

Children at Christmastime Around the World

Text by

Robina Beckles Willson

HEINEMANN : LONDON

Contents

William Heinemann Ltd
10 Upper Grosvenor Street, London W1X 9PA
LONDON MELBOURNE TORONTO
JOHANNESBURG AUCKLAND

First published 1983
Text © Robina Beckles Willson 1983
Illustrations © Satomi Ichikawa 1983
434 94361 4

Printed in Italy

Also illustrated by
Satomi Ichikawa
Under the Cherry Tree
Playtime
Let's Play
From Morn to Midnight
Friends
A Child's Book of Seasons

Colour origination by Imago Publishing Ltd

Foreword

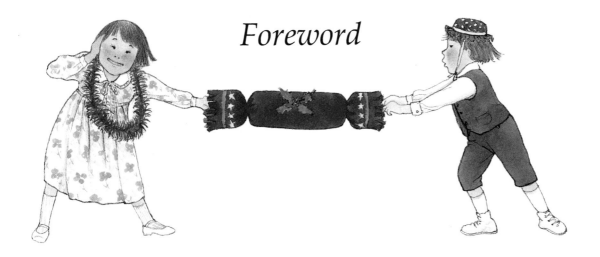

Christmas is a time of joyous celebration – a time to reunite with old friends and gather the family together, a time to delight in all the joys this special season can bring. Above all, Christmas is the time to remember and rejoice in the birth of the Holy Child in Bethlehem nearly two thousand years ago.

Almost every country has its own special Christmas traditions and throughout December children all over the world prepare for the Christmas festivities in their own special way. You are invited to share in some of their preparations described in this book. Enjoy your own traditions and create new ones and, above all, rejoice and have a Merry Christmas!

Before the celebrations begin, read the story of the first Christmas as it is acted out in nativity plays by children in many lands. Then find out about Christmas in different countries – and at the end of the book join in a wonderful party for children from all over the world.

The Story of Christmas

A long, long time ago, a woman named Mary lived in Nazareth. One day, an angel called Gabriel appeared to her and said, "God has sent me to speak to you, Mary."

"But why would an angel come to visit a poor woman like me?"

"Do not be afraid, Mary. God is pleased with you. He has chosen you to be blessed with the birth of His son. You are to call him Jesus."

Mary answered, "But I am to marry Joseph. He will be my husband."

"But this baby will not be Joseph's son: He will be the son of God," Gabriel told her.

Mary knelt down and said, "I accept what God has decided, and I look forward to the birth of my son."

Mary told Joseph about the angel's visit. "I wish I could stay here in Nazareth until my baby is born."

"We cannot disobey the Emperor of Rome," said Joseph. "He has ordered that each man must return to the place of his birth to be taxed. So we must go to Bethlehem, where I was born."

"It is far to Bethlehem?" Mary asked him.

"No, and we will take the journey slowly. My donkey is steady, and you will not have to walk and tire yourself."

"How strange it is that I should be the mother of the son of God."

"And that a poor carpenter like me should be chosen to be His earthly father," Joseph added.

When Joseph and Mary reached Bethlehem she was very tired. "Soon my child will be born," she told Joseph, "and we must find shelter for us all."

"Don't worry," he said. "I shall find somewhere to spend the night. I'll try this inn." So Joseph asked the innkeeper's wife, "Have you a room, please, for my wife and . . ."

"Not a single one. We've had no rooms for days with all these visitors. Try the inn down the road."

But at that inn there was no room either. All the inns were full. Then Joseph spoke to a little girl standing nearby. "Do you live in Bethlehem?"

"Yes, my parents have an inn. They are very busy with all their guests."

"Do you have room there for us? You see, my wife, Mary, is going to have a baby, and needs to rest after our long journey from Nazareth."

"Poor lady," said the girl. "Our own rooms are full, too, but perhaps my mother would let you use our stable. The donkey and cow live there, but it is clean and warm and dry."

"Thank you," said Joseph. "God must have sent you to help us. Lead us to your mother and the stable."

The mother and her daughter made room in the stable for Joseph and Mary. They were glad to rest there peacefully.

When Mary's baby was born she remembered what Gabriel had told her, and called her son Jesus.

In the fields near Bethlehem, some shepherds were guarding their sheep. They had to stay awake through the night to make sure that wild beasts did not hurt their flock.

Suddenly the angel Gabriel appeared. He shone so brightly in the darkness that they were alarmed. "Do not be afraid," said Gabriel. "I have come to bring you good news. Today, a Saviour, who is Christ the Lord, has been born in Bethlehem."

"You will find the baby wrapped in swaddling clothes, and lying in a manger. I have set my star in the sky to show you the way."

Then many angels sang with Gabriel. "Glory to God in the highest, peace on earth and goodwill to men."

As the shepherds hurried to Bethlehem, the star moved in the sky, showing them the way. When they saw Jesus in the stable they knelt down and praised God.

Some days later three kings from the East came to see Jesus in the stable. They had travelled far, guided by a bright star in the night sky.

The three kings brought gifts for the baby. One king presented Him with gold, another with frankincense, and the third with myrrh.

When they knelt in front of the baby, lying in the manger, they told Joseph and Mary that Jesus would be a king. "He has been born in the city of King David. But he will not be like any other king."

"Perhaps he will be the king of heaven," said Mary. She was thinking of the angel Gabriel, who had first told her about Jesus.

The shepherds and the three kings were delighted that they had found the baby Jesus. Ever since that time, people all over the world have remembered his birthday, and called it Christmas. They have rejoiced as the shepherds did. And they have given presents, just as the three kings did to the baby in the manger.

Christmas for the Animals

Animals are part of Christmas celebrations in many countries. There are many stories told about the friendly animals in the stable where Jesus was born.

It is said that the cow did not eat the fresh hay which was put in the manger, so that Mary could use the hay for the baby's bed. The cow also helped to keep the Holy Child warm by breathing on Him and warming Him with her breath.

The sheep gave Mary some wool so that she could weave a soft blanket, while the doves cooed Jesus to sleep.

Not only the shepherds were pleased to see Jesus. A robin sheltering in the stable roof sang for joy with the angels. Because it was the first bird song Jesus heard, He rewarded the robin by

making its voice sweeter still, and especially so in winter, at Christmastime.

A very small brown beetle crept into the stable that joyful night. When at last it reached the manger, only Jesus noticed the beetle, because it was so small. But Jesus touched it with His finger. And ever since then the glow-worm has shone with a tiny light, to guide travellers through the dark night.

It is also told that on Christmas Eve, at midnight, every farm animal has been given the gift of human speech. It is bad luck to disturb them, however, so no one has even reported overhearing them.

Even the bees are said to give homage to the Christ Child, by humming a psalm. "Give thanks to Him and bless His name," they sing in remembrance of the baby who was born in a manger.

Around the World to Church

All around the world on Christmas Eve people come together in love and friendliness to rejoice in the birth of the Holy Child. Bells begin to ring, calling Christians to church, to celebrate His memory once again. Families and friends attend midnight mass or other Christmas

services. Whether in a huge cathedral or a small chapel, all gather together to commemorate Christ's birth centuries ago.

Many will be singing one of the best-loved of all Christmas carols, "O Little Town of Bethlehem".

Now, join in with children all over the world as they prepare for the festive season and look forward to the celebrations of Christmas Day.

O Little Town of Bethlehem

O lit-tle town of Beth-le-hem, How still we see thee lie! A-

bove thy deep and dream-less sleep The si-lent stars go by. Yet

in thy dark streets shi-neth The ev-er-last-ing light; The

hopes and fears of all the years Are met in thee to-night.

O morning stars, together
Proclaim the holy birth,
And praises sing to God the King,
And peace to men on earth;
For Christ is born of Mary,
And, gathered all above,
While mortals sleep, the angels keep
Their watch of wond'ring love.

How silently, how silently
The wondrous gift is given!
So God imparts to human hearts
The blessings of His heav'n.
No ear may hear His coming;
But in this world of sin,
Where meek souls will receive Him, still
The dear Christ enters in.

O Holy Child of Bethlehem,
Descend to us, we pray;
Cast out our sin, and enter in,
Be born in us today.
We hear the Christmas angels
The great glad tidings tell.
O come to us, abide with us,
Our Lord Immanuel.

Great Britain and
United States of America

Great Britain and the United States share many Christmas customs from different lands.

On December evenings, parties of children go out to sing carols to neighbours and friends. As they knock at each door, they are welcomed in and given something delicious to eat and a warm drink.

A German tradition observed in both Britain and the United States is that of decorating the Christmas tree. The whole family helps to trim the tree, with candles or small electric lights, shining ornaments and tinsel.

Most families have a festive dinner on Christmas Day which they often share with grandparents, aunts and uncles, cousins, or friends. Delicious foods are prepared, among them roast turkey and Christmas pudding or mince pies.

The Christmas pudding is often made months beforehand and sometimes children help stir the mixture and make a wish as they do

it. Before the pudding is brought in, brandy is poured over it and then it is set on fire so that the pudding comes to the table flaming.

Many British and American homes are decorated with holly at Christmastime. This legend about the holly bush explains why.

When the shepherds hurried away to see the baby Jesus in the stable, they did not see that a tiny lamb came after them. Weak and ill, it followed the little shepherd boy who had been caring for it.

The lamb's bleating was too faint to be heard, so that no one picked it up to carry it. It stumbled on rough ground, and scratched itself on prickly holly bushes. But at last the lamb reached the stable and found the shepherd boy.

Mary saw the boy pick up the lamb and warm it in his

cloak. "My son will be kind to creatures smaller than himself, just as you are," Mary told the boy. "Your kindness to that little lamb will always be remembered."

And so every winter the berries on the holly bushes are bright red to remind us of that lamb with its scratches and the comfort given to it by a boy with kind ways.

The mistletoe plant with its white berries is also part of Christmas celebrations, especially in England. It has long been a symbol of friendship. In olden times, if friends met under mistletoe, they thought it would bring them good luck. If enemies did so, they stopped fighting. Today, when mistletoe is brought indoors, anyone standing beneath it can expect to be kissed.

On Christmas Eve, it is the custom for both British and American children to hang stockings over the fireplace or at the ends of their beds. Sometimes they write to Santa Claus or Father Christmas beforehand to tell him what they would like for Christmas.

It is hard to go to sleep on Christmas Eve, but Santa Claus won't come until everyone does. When he does arrive, it will be in a sleigh, pulled by reindeer with tinkling bells on their harness. He may come down the chimney or somehow sneak into the house another way. In any case, he always manages to fill the children's stockings before Christmas morning.

Santa Claus – or Father Christmas – and his reindeer ride through the sky on Christmas Eve. American children say he looks like this; British children think he wears a long red robe.

Silent Night
Austrian Carol

Si – lent night, Ho – ly night, All is calm, all is bright;

'Round yon vir – gin mo-ther and child, Ho-ly in-fant so ten-der and mild,

Sleep in heavenly peace,—— sleep in heavenly peace.

Silent night, Holy night,
Shepherds quake at the sight;
Glories stream from heaven afar,
Heav'nly hosts sing Alleluia!
Christ the Saviour is born!
Christ the Saviour is born!

Silent night, Holy night,
Son of God, love's pure light;
Radiance beams from Thy holy face,
With the dawn of redeeming grace,
Jesus, Lord at Thy birth,
Jesus, Lord at Thy birth.

Germany

In Germany, children start getting ready for Christmas at the beginning of December with Advent calendars. Advent means "coming" and it is the time when people prepare for the coming of Christ.

As with other birthdays, it is exciting to count the days up to the birthday of Christ. An Advent calendar has twenty-four numbered doors to open, one for each day of December up to Christmas Eve. Inside each door is a Christmas picture.

Another kind of Advent calendar is made of a wreath of fir branches on which twenty-four little boxes are hung. Each box, wrapped in brightly-coloured paper, has a number on the outside and a tiny present inside. One box is opened on every day of Advent.

Other children will help make an Advent wreath of fir branches bound together to make a circle. This is decorated with four red or yellow candles, set into metal cups. One candle is lit on the first

Sunday of Advent, two on the second, and so on up to Christmas Day.

In some parts of Germany children write to the Christ Child, asking for presents.

To make the letters sparkle and catch the Christ Child's eye as He passes, the children sprinkle the envelopes with sugar. They spread a little glue on to each one, then, while it is still sticky, they shake sugar on to it. The glittering envelopes are left on the window sill, and the children go to bed on Christmas Eve, hoping for presents the next day.

Sometimes on Christmas Eve presents are given secretly. While the family is settled at home, the door is suddenly pushed open just wide enough for small presents to be tossed inside on to the floor. Each member of the family opens a package to find inside another package bearing the name of someone else. Packages are passed back and forth until at last each gift reaches the person for whom it was intended. No one must ever find out who sent the presents, for that brings bad luck!

For German children, one of the most exciting moments of the holiday is Christmas Eve, when they see their Christmas tree for the first time. It is usually decorated secretly by the mother of the family.

One traditional German story often told on Christmas Eve is about a woodman and his family. As they sat snugly by the fire, they heard a knock at the door. They were surprised to see a small boy standing outside in the snowy forest, all by himself. So they took him in, and gave him warm food and drink and a bed for the night.

The next morning they were awakened by singing. It was a choir of angels, whose presence filled the cottage with light.

The woodman and his family realised then that they had given shelter to the Christ Child.

"You cared for me," said Jesus. "This will remind you of my visit." He touched a little fir tree near the door. "May this tree glow to warm your hearts. And may it carry presents, so that you are as kind to one another as you were to me."

Another well-loved story tells how a widow was secretly decorating a tree for her children. When she had gone to bed, spiders spun their webs all over it. The Christ Child, passing by, turned the webs to silver, to delight them all on Christmas morning. That is why we put tinsel on our trees.

The Netherlands

Saint Nicholas is the patron saint of all children. In Holland, the Dutch name for him is *Sinter Klaas,* which has become Santa Claus in Britain and the United States.

Nicholas was a bishop. He was a kind man, who liked to do good secretly. One day, he heard that a merchant had become so poor that he had no money to give to his three daughters when they were married. So Saint Nicholas crept up on to the roof of their house in the night and dropped three bags of gold down the chimney.

In the morning, the three sisters found the gold in the stocking they had hung up to dry.

This legend explains why children hang up stockings at Christmas, in the hope that Santa Claus will fill them with presents.

In Holland, December 6th is Saint Nicholas's own day. It is said that he sails to the city of

Amsterdam in a boat from Spain. With him travels his servant, Black Peter. Church bells ring as Saint Nicholas comes ashore. He wears a bishop's red robes and looks rather like Santa Claus. He rides a white horse and leads a colourful procession into the city to meet the queen.

Black Peter holds Saint Nicholas's horse. Dutch children are told that Black Peter keeps a record of what they do in a big book. Good children will be given presents, but Black Peter will chase the naughty ones with his stick.

Sometimes Saint Nicholas and Black Peter ride over the roof tops to give out presents to children. Often Dutch children put their clogs or shoes by the fireplace, hoping that Saint Nicholas will drop presents down the chimney. If they fill the clogs with hay and carrots for Saint Nicholas's horse, Saint Nicholas will also leave them some good things to eat.

Saint Nicholas or *Sinter Klaas* parties are sometimes held on Christmas Eve instead of the Saint's day, December 6th. Poems are written (often teasing ones) to other members of the family and no

one is meant to know who sends them as they are all signed "From *Sinter Klaas*".

A verse like this could be sent by a little girl to her brother:

Who is no help with the chores?
Who always forgets to shut doors?
I can't give his name.
Mine is almost the same.
If you must know – please ask Santa Claus.

There is also a treasure hunt for presents, with poems providing the clues. Gifts are wrapped and carefully hidden. The children then have to follow a trail of clues to find their presents. All these little gifts come from Saint Nicholas.

On this evening, the family usually have a special cake called a *letterbanket* or letter cake, made of marzipan and pastry. There is either one large cake in the shape of the first letter of the family name, or smaller initial cakes for each member of the family.

Letterbanket

1 lb/400 gm. packet of frozen puff pastry
8 oz/200 gm. packet of marzipan
One egg, beaten. Water.
Preheat oven to 425°F (200°C) or Gas 7

Thaw the puff pastry until it is soft. Roll it
out in a strip about 4 cm./1½ in. wide and
2 cm./¾ in. thick. Roll the marzipan into
sausages 1 cm./½ in. wide. Lay this on the
pastry and fold the pastry round the
marzipan. Stick the seam together by
brushing water on it and smoothing with
the fingers.

   Cut off lengths, and shape them to the
letters you want, sealing the ends. Put the
letters on a greased baking sheet, seams side
down. Brush them with beaten egg. Cook
for 25-30 minutes.

   One large family initial can be made
instead of little letters. For this, roll the
pastry to about 10 cm./4in. wide.

The Sinter Klaas Party

Poland and Czechoslovakia

Polish children watch the sky carefully on Christmas Eve, waiting for a sign of the first star. When it appears, usually at about six o'clock, the family can begin their feast. Before they start to eat, a thin bread wafer called an *oplatek* is passed around the table. The wafer has a picture of Mary and Joseph with the baby Jesus stamped on it. Each person breaks off a little piece of the *oplatek*. In the country, pieces used to be given to the farm animals as well. Even today the family pets may be allowed in to share the food.

Hay is spread on the floor and even under the tablecloth. This is to

remind everybody that Jesus was born in a stable. Traditionally, two empty places are left at the table, in case Mary should arrive with the baby Jesus.

When the meal is over, the children can open their presents.

Children in Czechoslovakia also watch the evening sky on December 6th. They are waiting for Saint Nicholas who is said to come down with a bag of presents and a bag of sticks. When the children think they can hear Saint Nicholas coming, they hurry to the table and say their prayers, hoping for a good reward.

A place will be left free at the table in case the Christ child should join the party.

Rocking

Czech Carol

Lit-tle Je-sus, sweet-ly- sleep, do not- stir;

We will- lend a- coat of- fur, We will rock you,

rock you, rock you, We will rock you, rock you, rock you,

See the fur to keep you warm, Snug-ly- round your ti-ny form.

Mary's little baby, sleep, sweetly sleep, We will rock you, rock you, rock you:
Sleep in comfort, slumber deep; We will serve you all we can,
We will rock you, rock you, rock you, Darling, darling little man.

Finland

The morning of Christmas Eve is a busy one for many children in Finland. That is when they go out to get their Christmas tree. They may have chosen it earlier, before the deep snow fell. Once it has been cut down, they bring it home on a sled. The tree must now be decorated in time for the evening party.

As busy as they are, the children in Finland do not forget birds and animals who might be starving in freezing wintry weather. They give the birds and animals their own "little Christmas". A farmer may contribute a sheaf of corn which is put on a tree for the birds to peck at, as you can see in the picture on the next page. Nuts are sometimes strung up in bags or chains. Or pieces of suet are hung from tree branches or from a tall pole stuck into the ground.

When the animals have been fed, the children will wait indoors where it is warm for Father Christmas to visit them on Christmas Eve. It is said that he comes to them from Lapland over the snow in a sleigh pulled by reindeer.

Special Christmas foods in Finland are cold ham or salted meat and pickled herrings, eaten with turnips, carrots and salted cucumbers.

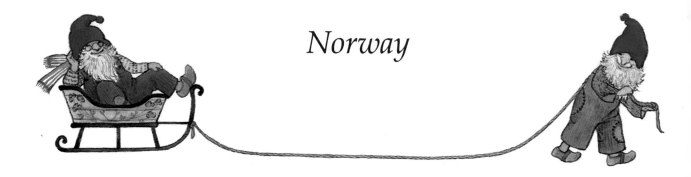

Norway

In Norway Christmas preparations begin early in December, when families start their Christmas baking. Many different kinds of biscuits and cakes are made as well as a rich Christmas bread called *julekake*, filled with raisins, candied peel and cardamom. The heat of all the ovens at this time is supposed to make the first heavy snows of winter melt.

At Christmastime Norwegian children also remember the Nisse, a little gnome who guards the farm animals. They put a bowl of special porridge out for this small Father Christmas. If they forget, he may play tricks on them.

Gingerbread is very popular in Norway at Christmas.
Here is a recipe for Gingerbread House Biscuits.

1½ oz/40 gm. margarine
4½ oz/120 gm. caster sugar
3 oz/70 gm. golden syrup
3 tbsp./50 ml water
10 oz/250 gm. plain flour

1 tsp. cinnamon
1 tsp. ground ginger
1 tsp. ground cloves
1 tsp. bicarbonate of soda

Mix the margarine, sugar and syrup in a bowl with a wooden spoon. Blend together the water, three spices and bicarbonate of soda, then put that into the bowl. Mix well and add the flour, working it all into a dough. Cover this with a damp cloth for at least half a day.

Preheat the oven to 425°F (220°C) or Gas 7. Roll out the dough on a floured board to about ¼ in./5 mm. thick. Then cut into shapes of houses. Roll up and re-use left-overs.

Lift your houses on to a greased baking tray with a fish slice, then bake them for 5-10 minutes, until they turn brown.

Leave them to set for a few minutes, then cool on a wire tray.

You can draw windows and doors on your cold biscuits with icing, made from 1 oz/25 gm. icing sugar beaten with a little egg white. You would need an icing bag and nozzle for this. Or you can make one by twisting some strong brown paper into a cone. Snip a tiny hole at the pointed end, fill the cone with icing and let it drip out to form the design.

Sweden

In Sweden, December 13th is a special day for this is the feast of Saint Lucia, whose goodness is remembered every year in towns and villages all over the country.

Lucia was an early follower of Jesus. In those days, Christians were sometimes cruelly treated. They met to pray to Jesus, hiding in underground caves. Lucia took them food secretly, in the night, so that they would not go hungry. On her head she wore a crown of candles. In this way, with both hands free to carry the food and drink, she was able to see her way in the dark.

One day, she was caught and killed by the Roman Emperor's men. But her kindness has never been forgotten and her story continues to bring brightness to the long dark winter nights.

Many Swedish children begin thinking of Saint Lucia on December 12th, when they cook special Lucia buns and ginger snaps. The next morning all the children get up early and the youngest girl dresses up as Saint Lucia in a long white dress with a red sash. Her brothers may act as "Star Boys", in white shirts. On the girl's head will be a

crown of evergreens with candles in it to light her way in the darkness, just like brave Saint Lucia. In her hands she carries a tray of coffee and Lucia buns to her family while they are still in bed.

Today, Swedish children often have a billy goat made of straw to guard the Christmas tree. He keeps away wicked spirits.

Even before Jesus was born, straw seemed to some to have magical properties. Farmers, for instance, spread it over fields to make crops grow better. Because the baby Jesus lay in a manger on straw, people began to use it for Christmas decorations to remember His birth in a stable. Swedish children often make straw decorations to hang on the Christmas tree. Other popular Christmas tree ornaments are little heart-shaped baskets which can be filled with sweets.

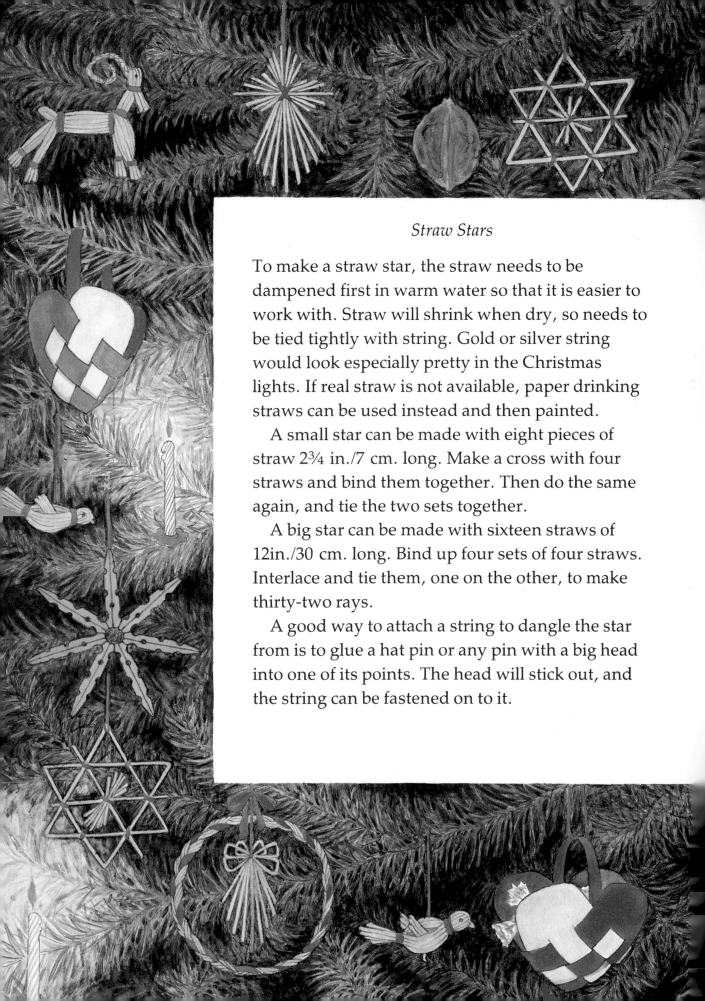

Straw Stars

To make a straw star, the straw needs to be dampened first in warm water so that it is easier to work with. Straw will shrink when dry, so needs to be tied tightly with string. Gold or silver string would look especially pretty in the Christmas lights. If real straw is not available, paper drinking straws can be used instead and then painted.

A small star can be made with eight pieces of straw 2¾ in./7 cm. long. Make a cross with four straws and bind them together. Then do the same again, and tie the two sets together.

A big star can be made with sixteen straws of 12in./30 cm. long. Bind up four sets of four straws. Interlace and tie them, one on the other, to make thirty-two rays.

A good way to attach a string to dangle the star from is to glue a hat pin or any pin with a big head into one of its points. The head will stick out, and the string can be fastened on to it.

Heart Baskets

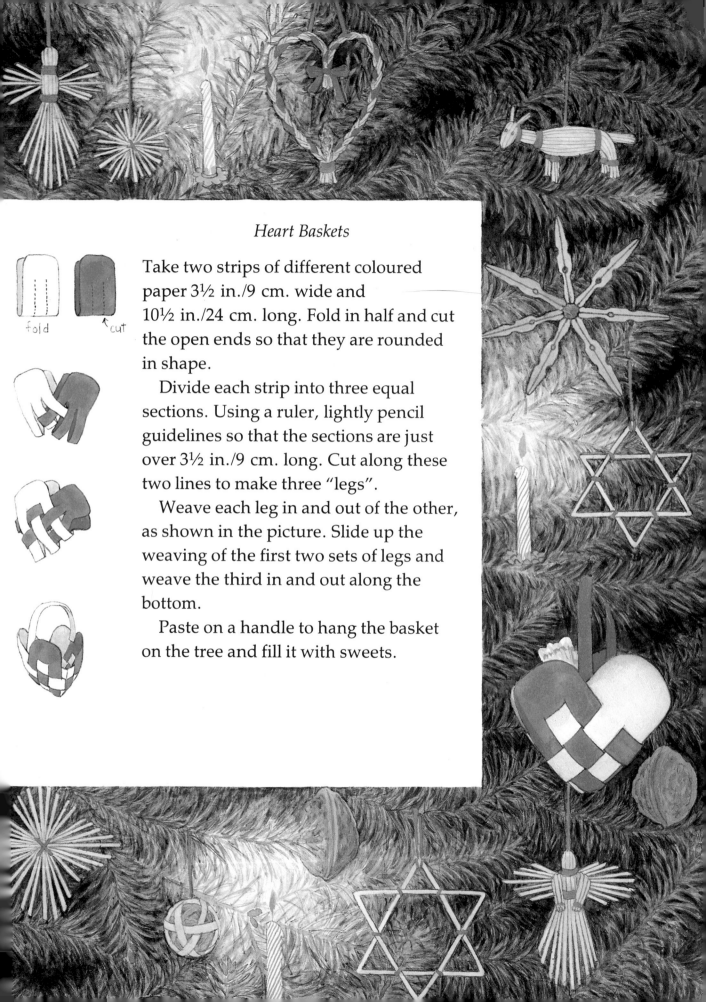

Take two strips of different coloured paper 3½ in./9 cm. wide and 10½ in./24 cm. long. Fold in half and cut the open ends so that they are rounded in shape.

Divide each strip into three equal sections. Using a ruler, lightly pencil guidelines so that the sections are just over 3½ in./9 cm. long. Cut along these two lines to make three "legs".

Weave each leg in and out of the other, as shown in the picture. Slide up the weaving of the first two sets of legs and weave the third in and out along the bottom.

Paste on a handle to hang the basket on the tree and fill it with sweets.

Russia

A Russian Christmas legend explains why, in the olden days, Russian children found black bread in their Christmas stockings.

Baboushka was an old woman who always welcomed travellers passing by her cottage. One winter morning, three richly dressed strangers asked for food and shelter. Baboushka kindly gave them black bread and tea, and let them sleep in her big bed.

When they awoke, Baboushka asked why they travelled at night.

"We are three kings from the East, following a star," they answered. "It is pointing the way to the Christ Child."

"I should love to go with you," said Baboushka.

But Baboushka did not want to leave before she had tidied her house, so she followed the kings later, carrying with her a gift of "black bread".

It took her months of travelling to reach Bethlehem and when she finally got there only the animals were left in the stable. Baboushka put her bread in the manger, so the Christ Child would know she had been there.

That night, a voice woke her saying, "I am the Christ child. Take my hand and come with me." Baboushka closed her eyes and then, smiling, went to Heaven that night.

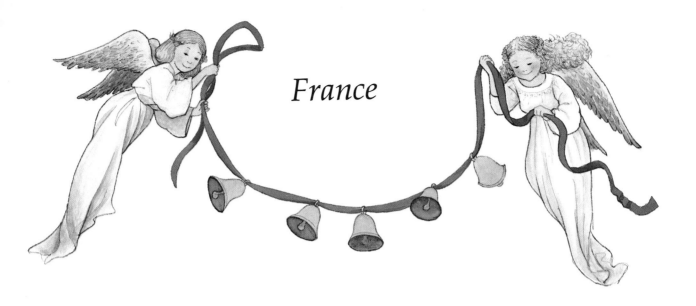

France

A crèche or crib is often found in French homes, with small clay figures, standing for Joseph, Mary, Jesus, the shepherds, the three kings and the animals.

At Christmas time, French families sometimes burn a log of cherry wood as a yule log. They carry it to the house on Christmas Eve. Then it is lit. Wine may be sprinkled on the cherry wood log.

In France there is also a custom that the fire is left alight, candles burning, and food and drink on the table just in case Mary should pass that way with the Christ Child.

On Christmas Eve in France, as in so many other countries, children put their shoes out by the fireside for *Père Noël*, as they call Father Christmas, for him to fill with presents during the night.

Il Est Né le Divin Enfant

Il est né le di - vin En - fant, ~ Jou - ez hautbois ré - son - nez, mu - set - tes,

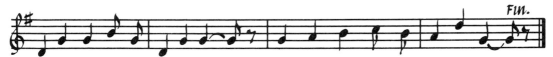

Il est né, le di - vin En - fant, ~ Chantons tous son a - vè - ne - ment! ~

Nous voi - ci dans cet heu - reux temps, An - non - cé par tous les pro - phè - tes

Nous voi - ci dans cet heureux temps, Ap - pe - lé de nos vœux ar - dents!

Italy

Saint Francis of Assisi has a special place in Christmas celebrations in Italy. He loved all living creatures and called animals his brothers and sisters.

Hundreds of years after Jesus was born, Francis visited Bethlehem, and saw the place where the stable had been.

The following Christmas, at home in Greccio in Italy, he decided to re-enact the story of the baby born in a manger. He did this to remind his people that Jesus was not rich, but born into a poor family, in a humble stable. He took a live ox and a donkey into a cave, and built a manger there, with wood and straw. Village people played the parts of Joseph, Mary and the shepherds. A little figure was carved of the baby Jesus.

Many people came, lighting their way with candles, to hear Francis tell the story of Jesus's birth. One man thought he saw the baby open his eyes when Francis looked into the manger.

Other churches in Italy copied Saint Francis's idea for a Christmas crèche. Then Italian families began making crèches in their own homes, and now families in countries all over the world have taken up this custom.

An old custom for Italian children is to go before Christmas from house to house playing songs on shepherds' pipes, and wearing shepherds' sandals and hats. They are given money to buy Christmas food.

But on Christmas Eve, Italians do without food for a whole day. Then, that night, after a midnight service, they have as grand and delectable a feast as they can manage which will include the special Italian Christmas cake called *panetone.*

Italian children have to wait for their Christmas presents until Twelfth Night, the Epiphany. This is when the three kings arrived in Bethlehem to worship the Christ Child. That night, children wait for the good witch, *la Befana*, to come down the chimney. Bad children find pieces of charcoal in their shoes, but good ones find presents.

58

Greece

In Greece, on Christmas Eve, boys often go out caroling in the streets. They beat drums and tap triangles as they sing. If they sing well they may be given money or nuts, sweets and dried figs to eat.

Sometimes a group of children decorate model boats with gold-painted nuts, which they carry as they go from house to house. This is an old custom which children in the Greek islands still enjoy.

Torches

Spanish Carol

Torch - es, torch - es, run with torch - es
All the way to Beth - le - hem! —————
Christ is born and now lies sleep - ing;
Come and sing your song to him! —————

Ah, ro - ro, ro - ro, my baby,   Sing, my friends, and make you merry,
Ah, ro - ro, my love, ro - ro;   Joy and mirth and joy again;
Sleep you well, my heart's own darling, Lo, he lives, the King of heaven,
While we sing you our ro - ro.   Now and ever more. Amen.

Mexico

In many parts of the world children act out the story of Christmas in nativity plays. In Mexico, children like to perform the part of the story where Mary and Joseph look for an inn to spend the night. They dress up for a procession called a *posada*, which is the Spanish word for "inn" or "lodgings".

There are nine *posadas*. The first one is on December 16th. Houses are decorated with evergreens, moss and paper lanterns. A board is made to carry painted clay figures of Mary, riding on a donkey, Joseph, and sometimes an angel guarding them as well.

Children are given lighted candles, and sent off in a procession, carefully holding the board with the clay figures on it. They call at the houses of neighbours and friends, and stop to sing outside. The song asks for shelter for weary Joseph and Mary. But the children are told there is no room at the inn, and that they must go away.

They try other houses until at last they find the *posada* where they are made welcome. Doors are opened and the children say prayers of thanks with the innkeepers. After that there is a party, with delicious things to eat and fireworks to watch.

The last of the *posadas* is on Christmas Eve. This time there will be a little manger on the board, and perhaps a stable and shepherds as well.

After the *posada* has been found and the prayers said, a figure of the baby Jesus is put into the manger. Families then go to midnight mass to welcome the birth of Jesus. And once again, after the quiet prayers, there are noisy fireworks. Church bells are also rung to announce that Christmas has arrived.

There is an old story told about a little Mexican girl on Christmas Eve. She was so poor she had no money to buy a present to take to the crib in the church. Sadly, she stood outside the church door and watched other people carrying in their gifts.

A stone angel stood nearby, almost hidden by tall weeds. The little girl started to clear them away. Suddenly, she heard a voice, saying, "Take these weeds into the church and the Christ Child will bless them and you."

She gathered an armful of weeds, went into the church and up to the crib. As she walked, the leaves at the top of each stem turned bright red, just as if they had burst into flame.

Since then these flowers have been grown specially for Christmas and given the name Poinsettia. But some people call them Fire Flowers of the Holy Night in memory of the miracle.

Mexican children receive their presents after Christmas, on January 6th, the feast of the Three Kings. But they also have

other treats through the Christmas festival. The most unusual one is the *piñata*. *Piñatas* are decorated clay jars usually in the shapes of birds and animals, and filled with presents and good things to eat.

The game is played each evening after the *posada* prayers. The *piñata* is hung up by a string from a tree or anywhere else it can swing freely. Children are blindfolded, and then take turns tapping at the *piñata* with a stick until it splits open. When it does, there is a scramble for the gifts that come spilling out.

You can make your own *piñatas* for a Christmas party with balloons. Blow up a balloon, then hang it up by a piece of string. This can now be covered with papier-mâché.

To make papier-mâché cut or tear newspaper strips about 5cm./2in. wide. Cover these with very wet wallpaper paste and then set these down in overlapping strips around the balloon until it is completely covered. This is a messy procedure, so do it in the kitchen or where you can spread out newspapers on a table. If you want a strong *piñata* to hold a lot of things, put on three or four paper strip layers.

Leave this to dry. Once the papier-mâché is firm and dry, cut a big enough hole in it for you to fill the *piñata*. Then, remove the popped balloon and fill the *piñata* with sweets and small unbreakable presents.

Now the *piñata* can be painted or decorated as you like.

India

The Indians who have become Christians have mixed together their own customs with those from other countries.

Instead of Christmas trees they decorate banana or mango trees. They may also decorate their houses with mango leaves.

In some parts of India small clay lamps burning oil are used as Christmas decorations. They are put out along the edges of flat roofs, or on the tops of walls.

Churches in India are decorated with bright red poinsettia plants and lit with candles for the special Christmas Eve service.

Japan

There are not many Japanese children who are brought up as Christians, but some of the customs of Christmas have been brought to Japan from the United States and other countries.

The children will at least enjoy Christmas carols, sending Christmas cards, and, most of all, giving and receiving Christmas presents. They feel that Christmas is a time to share their happiness.

Parties are held, with children playing games and dancing. The Japanese Christmas cake is a sponge cake, decorated with trees, flowers and a figure of Santa Claus, all made of creamy icing.

Australia

People have come to live in Australia from all over the world and have brought their own customs with them.

In Australia, Christmas comes in the middle of summer when the weather is very hot. Many Australians have a traditional British Christmas dinner with roast turkey followed by a rich Christmas pudding. Others may have cold turkey and salad at a picnic on the beach or in the country. Most Australian homes have decorated Christmas trees and evergreens as well.

Away in a Manger

A - way in a - man - ger, no - crib for a bed, The-
lit -tle Lord Je - sus laid down his sweet head. The
stars in the bright sky looked down where he lay, The
lit -tle Lord Je - sus a - sleep on the hay.

The cattle are lowing, the baby awakes,
But little Lord Jesus no crying he makes.
I love thee, Lord Jesus!
　　　　　　Look down from the sky,
And stay by my side
　　　　　　until morning is nigh.

Be near me, Lord Jesus; I ask thee to stay
Close by me for ever, and love me, I pray.
Bless all the dear children in
　　　　　　thy tender care,
And fit us for heaven
　　　　　　to live with thee there.

Preparing for the Party

So children around the world celebrate Christmas, but suppose all of the children in this book were to come to one grand party. Here are

some of the preparations that might be made for them. On the table would be a ham, a Christmas pudding, mince pies, biscuits, sweets and lots more delicious things to eat.

The Christmas Party